Forgetting Is
My Superpower

16 Poems and an Essay

Zahara Heckscher

Acknowledgements

Thanks to Anne Becker and the members of her Chapbook Class. To dreamweaver Yael Flusberg. To Dennis Brutus for allowing me to consider believing that poetry is important. To every person who has played the Poetry Game, especially the children, the old people, the crazies, and those who say they do not write poetry. To my students, for teaching me. To Zein El-Amine and editor Johnna Schmidt, with infinite gratitude. To Reb David for leaps of faith. To Roz Timberg for belief. To the Sisterhood for levitation. To my doctors and nurses for allowing me to live to this season. To Melinda St. Louis and all who walked with me. To Rock Creek Park and Malcolm X Park and the hawks and the drummers. To Ethelbert Miller for saying "Pay yourself first." To Lori Waselchuk, creative visionary and midwife. With deep gratitude to Aliyah Silver.

Mosaic details from the Irving Street mural of Columbia Heights, *Mutual Inner Peace*, designed and created by Arturo Ho with participants in the Latin American Youth Center Summer Program.
Design by Lori Waselchuk

www.zaharaheckscher.com

For my family, especially my son Max.

"The more we forget,
the happier we are."

David Spence

Contents

Poems

Plus

Poems

Forgetting

Amphibian memories of tadpole life
crawl out of muddy water in my brain
to warn me, but they have no words,
only images of strange fish with fangs
and feelings of familiar confusion, the confluence
of desire and repulsion.

Clear water is made obscure if
the past never settles to the bottom. Sometimes
memory is submerged under layers of mud
for good reason.

Those who cannot forget find it difficult to learn.
Yet learning to avoid fish requires frogs to remember.
Therefore, choose your memories with great care,
as much as a snake who lies next to a pond,
licking the air, waiting for tadpoles
to sprout legs and crawl.

Red Salamander

who can breathe under water
was once a star
before mist cooled to ocean
before molten rock cooled to earth
before the small circle of fire
spun off from the red sun

Is the Moon the Light or the Hole in the Center of the Light?

in the middle of the light is a space
a gap at the center
silence
play
sleep
pray

time to remember, reflect
time to forget

time to look at the marzipan moon while you wait for
the chai on the tray with the white clay pitcher of cream
and the silver bowl of sparkling sugar on the night porch
where you hear the waves crash and seep into the space
between the sand

El-Kamar, beloved, I forget what I was thinking when I
saw the moon rise outside the airplane window

El-Kamar, beloved, I forget what my mother said about
reading in the light of the moon

El-Kamar, beloved, I forget the sharp words that broke
on the corner of the crescent, that night when we ap-
proached the locked gate

El-Kamar, beloved, I wish to forget how it felt to touch
your face

Autobiography

I am she who seeks light
I have my grandma Frieda in me
her dark eyes peer out through mine.
I am not afraid of dancing.
I am not afraid of crossing
rivers without bridges
jumping from stone to stone.
When I was born, an angel
took away my black hair and
gave me a bag of golden dust.
When I die, I want the ancestors
to be able to say, she was a good Jew
and I want Frieda to be able to say
you were a good girl.

Tamale Dust

On Halloween night 1986, I
walked the bridge from Mexico to Texas
pesos turning into pennies in my pockets
halfway across the Rio Grande

Later, as the sun set, I
stood by the road, alone
tamale dust on my feet
my thumb in the gringo air

And my bones were filled
with fear of days of dead and
pumpkinless heads and
men with guns and
angry armadillos

But from the grey air came the
sound of a truck's horn
stopped a quarter mile ahead of me,
and my tamale dust feet carried me up
to a sober alcoholic
driving red desert sand
from Arizona to Carolina

For forty seven hours, we
traded travels, tales and stopped five times
for eggs, toast, and coffee, and
his truck protected me like
Madonna holding Jesus

The second of November 1986, he
gently set me down outside this city
and even now his
kindness sticks to my skin
like tamale dust on my old boots

San Francisco

summers are cold here
but spring comes in February
when the days alternate
sun rain sun rain
and the trees think they are
in heaven

The Berkeley Station Master

Through my shoes I felt the brown tiles shaking.
Through the glass she saw my hands shaking.
Through my hands I felt my heart shaking
like the core of the moon on the day the Apollo landed.

I wanted to learn about the sea of tranquility,
Salaam.
I wanted to learn about the smoothness of her silk scarf,
Hareer.
I wanted to learn about songs of comfort by Jerry Garcia
his calluses hard and polished
G, E, A, F sharp
amplified acoustics in round ripples
floating up from Haight Ashbury park
flying lyrics about the Gulf of Mexico
as seen from the tip of the slim silver sliver.

Zilzal, the floor trembled.
Filfil, my tongue tasted like pepper.
El-Asifa, a storm of sand cut off the light from my eyes.

The other passengers engaged in their daily waltz to work.
Zilzal did not slow them down.

Through my shoes I felt the brown tiles shaking.
Through the glass she saw my hands shaking.
Through my hands I felt my heart shaking
like the core of moon on the day the Apollo landed.

The station master steps out from the square glass booth.
She pats me on the back
like a mother patting her baby
and she chants
acha, acha, acha.

Salt a Bird

When I dreamt of Razyla, the yellow roses bloomed.
Strange for February, she said, in Altona.
Never such a gentle winter since 1663,
the year her great grandmother was born.

Razyla tossed a pinch of salt on the threshold every morning.
Her mother told her it would bring her a multitude of children.
As if each tiny crystal could turn into a dancing girl,
a set of twins, or three boys with dark brown eyes.

Razyla had eight children, the first a girl, Liza.
The great grandmother of my father.
Liza passed the story of the salt down the
path of generations, Altona to Hamburg
to Berlin and back to Hamburg.

The story changed in each generation:
Salt on the threshold
Salt on the front porch
Salt on the gate
Salt on the tail of the rooster on the gate.

Grandma Frieda gave my father a saltshaker.
If you can get salt on a pigeon's tail,
you'll get a brother or sister, she told him.
He never received a sibling:
His failure to salt a bird.
His first taste of sorrow.

Mary in Kiwiland

Forty years ago Mary gave me a toy koala
about as big as seven kiwis
made of kangaroo fur

Today she confuses me with my sister
thinks I live in Hawaii
calls me at three am

Mary's son moved from Wellington to West Australia
an ambulance driver
kangaroos jumping through his backyard

When I went to visit
I saw a real koala
ten times bigger than the toy
too big, I thought

Mary remembers Paul Robeson
She shows me a picture of him with her husband
Noa Nowalowalo, water in the waterfall
Fijian prince and freedom fighter

Now Noa is gone

Mary sits with her golden granddaughter
tells her stories of World War II
the whistle of a bomb falling
in the English countryside

Mary gets up to make a cup of tea
heating the pot with boiling water
the way her mother taught her
The tea tastes like Oxford in the summer of 1951
black tea with two spoons of milk
in her father's rose garden

Mary looks past the golden girl to Wellington Bay
and wonders where she is
how did she end up in Kiwiland?

River

For Ray Davis

I saw a river submerged under itself
drowning ducks, trees and even fish

I saw a tornado suck air from clouds
turning the sky green
leaving the flowers gasping

I saw an earthquake swallow itself
consuming boulders, hills, mountains
leaving the leveled plain without a scar

I saw a fire consume its own flame
red eating yellow, yellow eating red,
without touching the dry wood of the forest

I saw life live itself into ashes and dust
hurl itself down through time so fast
the angels could see the sparks
fly up to heaven

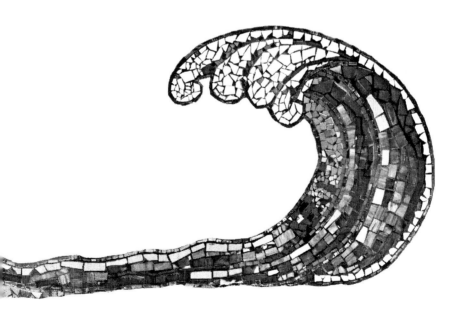

The Envoy

The bird is a mensh
His grandmother was from Mexico
A small forest just southeast of Cuernavaca
At the foothills of the mountain of the sleeping goddess
La montaña de la diosa dormida

The bird's name is Sheliyech
Messenger
Envoy
Carrier of truth from dreams that float above the forest
At the foot of the mountain
Where the goddess sleeps

The bird is a messenger
But he cannot speak our words
Not English nor Spanish nor Yiddish
Nor any of a thousand human tongues

But he sings his message each morning
When Penelope lifts the cloth from his cage
Embroidered with the colors of Mexico
Aqua, mustard, chili, hibiscus

He sings his message true
Sometimes serious, sometimes a joke
Like the *badchen* at the wedding in the old country
With striped socks
Of red and white

Sometimes he sings a perfect *bobe mayes*
A whistled tale of maidens, matchmakers, and magic

Sometimes he sings a tune for his nestlings
Eight hatchlings in the pet store
Small nest, large cage
Near the window where Penelope passed

Kinderlach, kinderlach, kinderlach
Penelope sometimes hears the yearning
Under the good cheer of the story
Like a *klezmer* tune
In a language she does not know
Or a *nigun* she hears out the window
Of the synagogue down the road
Where these days
Only old men *daven*

My love, my heart, my life
Mi amor, mi corazón, mi vida
She sings to Sheliyeh
Mi cariñoso amigo, mi paisano, mi enviado
And without the words to say it
She knows *koyech* is in the house
Eternal power of home

People Named After Dogs

Twenty three years ago
this spring, I hitchhiked
from Middletown to Newton
my new degree in hand
and arriving late afternoon I found
a black lab named Henry
outside my father's house.

Henry greeted me as if we had
met before. I could see
he was a good dear dog.
My father loved him.
But dad did not have enough time
for walks, and six months later
gave Henry to another family.
Dad felt alone without his companion.
He got a stuffed animal
a black lab named Henry
that gave him comfort.

When my father died
one year ago this spring
his beloved partner took that Henry
and gave my son a smaller Henry
the stuffed animal he sleeps with every night.
My sister is pregnant with a boy.
When asked the name, she says,
I think he will be Henry.

The Day Before My Sister Gave Birth

Here is how I would like to remember this day
A papaya lay sliced in two on a teal plastic mat
We lay holding hands under the silver fan
The breeze ruffled the curtains
Through the window we could see the yellow ohana
The green umbrella in the garden
The blue of the sky
A dog barked
Birds sang
Life called with irregular regularity
And we waited for the cry

Esperanza

No sé
porque
me siento que
todo esto es esperanza
esperando
hasta que
me encuentro un hombre
y el hombre me da un hijo
y el hijo me da un beso
y el beso me da la respuesta
a esta pregunta
que me pregunto

Waiting

I don't know why
I feel that
all this is waiting
and hoping
waiting
until
I find a man
and the man gives me a child
and the child gives me a kiss
and the kiss gives me an answer
to this question
I ask myself

The Oyster and the Goose

Is this what the oyster feels
after spitting out its pearl?
Or the goose
upon laying her first golden egg?

Surprise that so much dirt and guts and blood and pain
could produce a thing so smooth and bold.
Surprise, even after knowing
that this was the thing ever dreamed about
imagined, wished for
but never quite believed.

Surprise to find that despite
the rock-like proof of inner beauty
he is still an oyster;
she is still a goose.

Now that I have attained my dream
I understand God's little joke.
I am still an oyster;
I am still a goose.

Twenty-four on the H1 Bus

Twenty-four is not your prime
but I can see it from here.
You'll really hit your stride
around forty-five and then your friends
will wonder how it is that you
won't appear to age for fifteen years.

At twenty-four I also see the child you were,
so earnest that all the other children liked you
even though technically you
were not one of the popular ones.

In your smooth caramel skin
and your scarf and wool jacket
not quite matching I see that you will never
be fashionable per se but you will
continue to dress
with enough grace to please yourself.
Unlike some of us
you won't strive for more
in that department.
You'll put your energy
into more important things.

Today on your way to your second
week of work at a job you feel delighted
to have, you can just enjoy the pleasantness of being
on the bus on a chilly but sunny day.

Even in your eighties the same optimism
will show in the tipped up corners of your lips
and the light shining from within your eyes.

And you shall one day be blessed to know a rare pleasure:
Your children will know how lucky they are
and they will tell you so.

Plus

Forward at the End

Beloveds,

Forgetting is my superpower. In a family with so much pain through the generations, forgetting is a vital skill, a survival tactic, an act of resistance, a sign of health.

Yet I remember so much, so vividly. I remember the green and white dress of the slender girl, Loveness, standing in the field at the curve of the red dirt road outside Mkushi, Zambia, two decades before the new century broke. I remember how my toes felt when I jumped from pillow to pillow on the floor of the playroom in the house in Newton and how my fingers felt when I touched the wooden camel on the threshold above the fireplace. I remember the steam on the bowl of soup that Nicolasa placed on the table in Villa de las Flores, Colonia Ruben Jaramillo, and I remember Cuca's laugh when she first walked down the stairs to greet me.

Names, the color of a friend's eyes, the keys, I forget them all, of course, with mundane talent. My gift, my blessing, my grace is a conscious mind that excels at forgetting slights, jabs, meanness, conflicts, and, yes, even horrible happenings. As to my unconscious, I cannot attest. A few sharp corners still poke my nights.

Some of the harshest memories that remain are not my own but those given to me. I have tried not to include them here. Even when our collective survival, our tribal duty, or our sense of righteousness sometimes demand that we never forget, our healing can demand that we do -- selectively -- allow some details to float away. So these poems are not about what happened to the Heckschers of Hamburg, or the whistle in the sky above a boys' school in Reading. Most of that, I would like to forget. But even when my brain forgets, or when I chose not to pass on the stories, I have learned that some of the pain remains coiled in my DNA, and my DNA is in the poems, and the poems are part of what I pass on.

I think about how I want you, my beloveds, to remember me. Sometimes I worry that you will remember me thin and weak. But I want you to remember me standing my ground, calling out for justice until the police handcuff me and drag me away. I want you to remember me laughing as we walk on water with paddles. I want you to remember me listening to your poems as we sit in a circle in the living room.

Long time hence, when the facts of my life are forgotten, when my bones have turned to earth, when my books have turned to dust, perhaps some molecular ripples of my existence will continue to bounce, vibrate, intersect, cause and effect down the eras. I comfort myself that this is the form my memories will take, until the last Jew drinks the last glass of wine at the last Seder, until the daytime sunlight dims to darkness and the oceans all turn to ice.

Then, all our memories will be gone.

Or maybe they will live again on another distant planet that finds a way to listen to who we were.

Some of these poems are true. I really did hitchhike from the Mexican border to Washington, DC, walking across to bridge to Laredo, Texas on Halloween night of 1986. I really did think koalas were the size of my tiny stuffed animal until I saw a real koala at the Sydney zoo when I was about 36. The Berkeley station master really did come out of her booth to hug me during an earthquake.

But I took full advantage of my poetic license. So some of the poems are big blatant lies.

The lying poems tell the most truth.

This one is true: I really was born with a bag full of golden dust.

Glossary of Immigrant Words

I am the co-inventor of the Poetry Game and the Chief Poetic Officer of the Poetry Game Project. A few of the poems in the collection were written while playing the Poetry Game, including the Arabic, Yiddish, Spanish, and English versions. Some definitions of words used in the poems, in the order they appear:

Zilzal - (Arabic) Earthquake

Filfil - (Arabic) Pepper

El Asifa - (Arabic) Storm

Hareer - (Arabic) Silk

Salaam - (Arabic) Peace

El-Kamar, also spelled *Al Qamar* - (Arabic) The moon, or beloved

Acha, properly spelled *achha* or *achchha* - (Hindi) Literally means "good" but has many other meanings depending on context, from "Yes, go on" to "I understand." It is sometimes spoken to children while comforting them.

Koyech - (Yiddish) Strength

Seliyach - (Yiddish) Messenger, envoy

Kinderlach (Yiddish) - Dear children

Klezmer - (Yiddish) A Jewish music originating in the shtetls of Eastern Europe

Nigun - (Yiddish) A tuneless melody sung in Jewish groups as a sort of wordless musical prayer

Badchen - (Yiddish) An old fashioned Jewish itinerant entertainer and joker

Bobe mayes - (Yiddish) Old wives tales

Daven - (Yiddish) Pray

Mi cariñoso amigo, mi paisano, mi enviado - (Spanish) My affectionate friend, my compatriot, my messenger